A Mother's Assurance

Jessica A. Wiley

ENTEGRITY
CHOICE PUBLISHING

Entegrity Choice Publishing
POB 453, Powder Springs, GA 30127
info@entegritypublishing.com

This is a work of fiction. The views expressed in this work are solely those of the author and do not necessarily reflect the views of the publisher, and the publisher hereby disclaims any responsibility for them.

ISBN: 978-0-692-28050-8
ISBN: 978-0-9909397-5-7 (eBook)

Library of Congress Control Number: 2015954933

Printed in the United States of America

ENTEGRITY
CHOICE PUBLISHING

I was inspired to write "A Mother's Assurance" because I remember how insecure I was about my appearance as a child. Like many others, I was teased in school. This caused me to become self–conscious and even dislike the person God created me to be. I felt my lips were too big (I used to hold them in), my legs were too long and my forehead was huge. Even more upsetting was the fact that many of the women who were viewed as "beautiful" looked nothing like me.

With time and reassurance from my mother; I learned I was in fact beautiful just as I was. I learned God created me to look the way I did and that meant I was already perfect! Once I realized this I began to feel happy and free. I could not keep this good news to myself. I had to share it.

When our children believe they are beautiful, with their kinky hair, dark complexion, wide nose etc., the more accepting and loving they will be to themselves.

You are amazing inside and out.

Put a smile on your face and never doubt.
You are awesome in God's image you
are made. Hold your head up with pride,
come out of the shade.

While I'm at school, kids tease me.

They call me fat.

They say I'm ugly.

They say my face and body look funny.

Don't listen to others who are being mean.

Know that you are handsome, trust and believe.

You are made in the image of God.

Sweetheart, look in this mirror.
I'll tell you what I see.

I see a child that is smart and
as delightful as can be.

I see a child who is sharp,
handsome and cool.

I see a child who should be
proud going to school.

I see a smile and features made
just for you.

I see a beautiful angel who
God adores, too.

Kids point, laugh and call me names.

I wish I could disappear.
I feel ashamed.

Let's pray for kids, who aren't very nice.

Kindness will rub off on them before they can think twice.

You are amazing; you are made in the image of God.

My hair is coarse;
to me it seems kind of—short.

Coarse hair is not bad,
cheer up don't be sad.

You may wear it loose with big curls or small braids; enjoy your hair whatever the grade.

You are beautiful;
you are made in the image of God.

My head is oddly shaped.

If it were smaller,
that would be great.

Your head is just fine;
it's what's inside that defines.

You are good–looking;
you are made in the
image of God.

My eyes are big and round.

Is there a way I can slim them down?

Why try when you're the apple of God's eye?

You are handsome;
you are made in the image of God.

My nose is wide and flat.

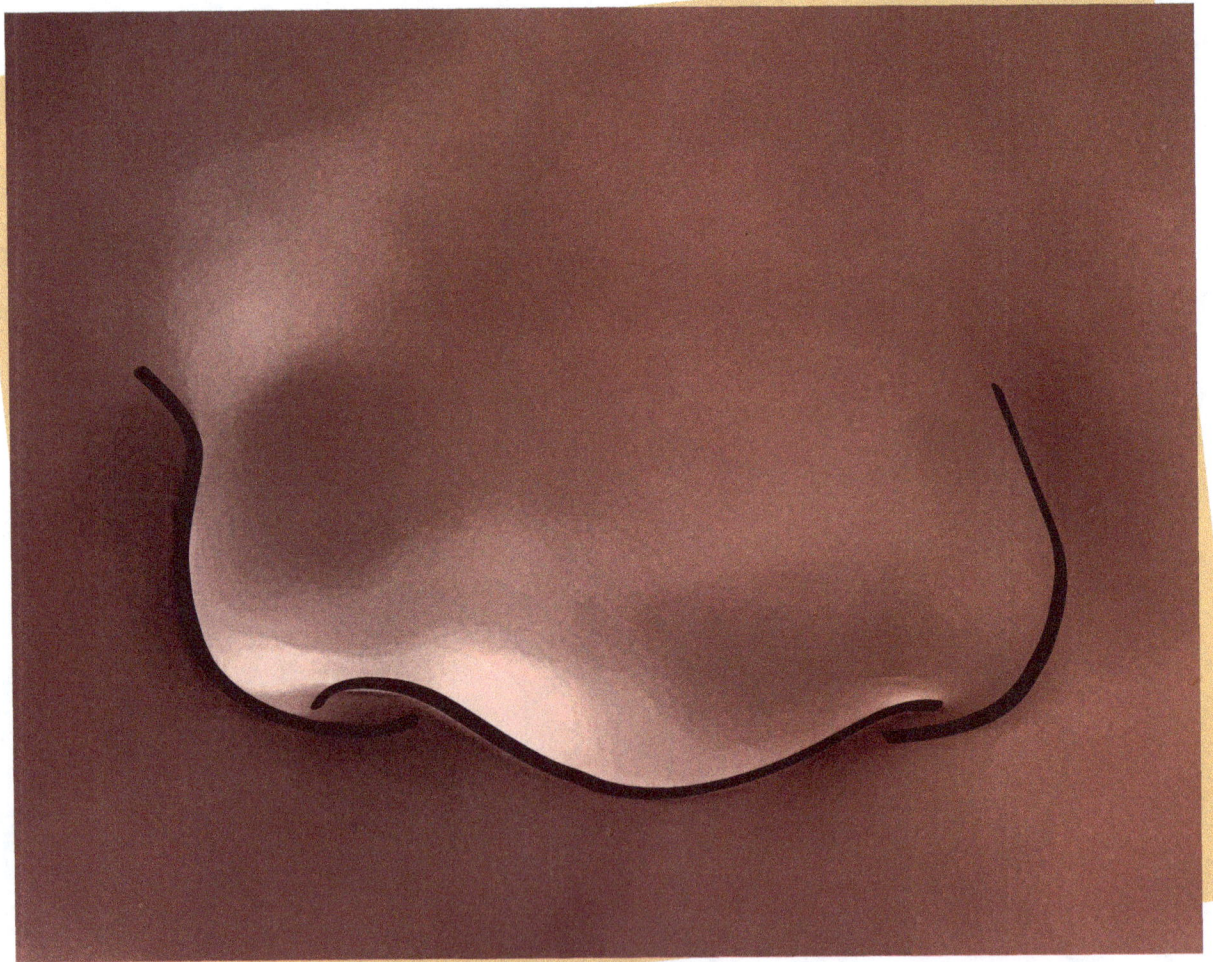

How I wish it wasn't like that.

Would you prefer pointy and light?

Everyone is different and that's alright.

You are unique; you are made in the image of God.

My lips are brown and full.

I 'll hold them in then I 'll look cool.

Lips come in all colors and shapes.

Don't hold them in;
your lips look great!

You are lovely;
you are made in the image of God.

I have
freckles
that take
up space.

How I
wish they
weren't on
my face.

Your freckles are a part of you.

Look! Mom has freckles, too.

You are beautiful;
you are made in the image of God.

My arms and legs are long and skinny.

I try to hide them, so I won't look silly.

Your arms and legs give
you much needed length.

Stand tall and smile your
shape is absolutely great!

You are beautiful;
you are made in the
image of God.

My tummy is not little.

Mommy, look how it jiggles.

Your tummy is full, more for me to tickle.

You know how I love to hear you giggle.

You are beautiful;
you are made in the image of God.

My feet are huge like Bozo's blues.

I wish I never had to take off my shoes.

You think your feet are very big.

You'll grow into them, just like I did.

You are beautiful; you are made in the image of God.

My skin is black.

That can't be right!

I'll wipe it off, so I can be bright.

Stop, put down the towel!

Your black skin is gorgeous, smooth and silky.

Some wish they look like you, don't try to change.

You are wonderfully and perfectly made!

You are amazing inside and out.

Put a smile on your face and never doubt.

You are awesome in God's image you're made.

Hold your head up with pride, come out of the shade.

About the Author

Jessica A. Wiley is a native of Chicago, Illinois. She obtained her bachelor's degree in English Literature from Governor's State University. In May 2009, she received her Masters of Divinity degree from the Interdenominational Theological Center (ITC) in Atlanta, Georgia.

As a child, Jessica was teased and as a result, she battled a variety of insecurities. Her book, "A Mother's Assurance" is her opportunity to reinforce and affirm to children that they are beautiful just as they are; no adjustments are needed.

Jessica resides in Atlanta, Georgia with her daughter Andrea.

ENTEGRITY
CHOICE PUBLISHING

P.O. Box 453
Powder Springs, Georgia 30127

info@entegritypublishing.com

eBook is available at
Amazon, Barnes and Noble, Google Play,
Apple iBooks and other online retailers.

www.ingramcontent.com/pod-product-compliance
Lightning Source LLC
Chambersburg PA
CBHW062012090426

42811CB00005B/829